LETTER

OF

GENERAL BENJ. F. BUTLER,

TO

HON. E. R. HOAR.

GIVES HIS OFFICIAL AND POLITICAL BIOGRAPHY, WITH A REPLY TO THE JUDGE'S IMPUTATIONS UPON THE GENERAL.

PUBLISHED BY REQUEST.
1876.

LETTER.

LOWELL, October, 1876.

JUDGE EBENEZER ROCKWOOD HOAR: —

DEAR SIR, — I have read with attention and careful consideration the remarks reported to have been made by you at a meeting of persons who assembled at Young's Hotel to defeat the nomination of the Republican convention of the Seventh District, in order to re-elect the Democratic incumbent, and also your letter accepting its nomination with that intention; and take leave to reply to some of your suggestions.

That such was the purpose of the meeting, I rely upon your own reported words: "If by using my name the result shall be that Gen. Butler shall be defeated, and if, knowing the sentiments of the people of the district, it is the opinion of gentlemen that it can be done, I should see no objection to it."

If there had been any purpose or hope expressed in that meeting of the election of even as uncertain and unreliable a Republican as Judge Hoar shew himself to be by his election of Mr. Tarbox to the present Congress, I should have felt it my duty in this crisis of public affairs, — of peril so imminent to good government and the peace of the country, — at least to have endeavored to do something, to make any concession, by which the honest, patriotic Republicans of this district could have found representation, and a Republican majority been secured in the House of Representatives.

But, quoting your words again, you say: "If you, gentlemen, consider that the best thing to do, and that you can *carry on the fight*, of which there is some reasonable prospect of success," then you are willing to allow your name to be used. This is conclusive that the movement is a mere personal "fight" upon me, and not in aid of the Republican party. Therefore I must accept the gage as it is thrown down, and meet a personal "fight" personally.

You say that "it [the fight] simply involves my submitting for the next thirty days, if I choose, to the abuse of Gen. Butler's speeches and 'The Traveller,' and such little organs as he owns and can buy, to an unlimited quantity of personal abuse."

Surely, Judge, I never have said any harsher things of the newspapers than that. You thus aver that newspapers can be bought for "unlimited personal abuse." I have believed and felt that for a long time of some newspapers, and I am glad to have the high authority of one intimately connected with, and so persistently puffed and boosted by the newspapers, for my belief. Don't be alarmed, Judge; from me you will receive no personal abuse, and I do not own a dollar in any newspaper, nor shall I buy one, even if otherwise inclined, now. Newspapers only make or mar little timid and shuffling men. You have disarmed me, for you say you will take no active part in the canvass. I cannot, therefore, meet you face to face before our neighbors; and after I subscribe my name to this communication, during the present canvass I promise you that I shall hardly make a personal allusion to you, except upon some new provocation. I never have made an unprovoked personal assault upon any one in a political canvass; or during my eight years' service in the House made such personal attack, as I think all my colleagues will bear me witness: and I may be permitted to say at the same time, that, when once attacked, the attack has been repelled in such manner that nobody has ever repeated the experiment.

If you had contented yourself with accepting a nomination, against the will of the Republican organization of the district, making no personal onslaught upon me, no word of unkind allusion to you, or other, except to bring your better qualities before your wished-for constituents, would have passed my lips, as has been the case in all my public utterances heretofore. The personal relations on which we have stood, as members of the bar, of the same party, and neighbors in the same county, constrained me to this, although I have been painfully aware of your political opposition to me ever since you so unceremoniously left the cabinet of President Grant.

You say, in your carefully prepared letter, written at Concord, in the peace and quiet of your home, where kindly thoughts, even of one's enemies, usually visit the most jaundiced mind, that you write it "with no personal hostility to Gen. Butler." If you can use such harsh language, make such unfounded accusations and such degrading imputations in regard to a man against whom you have no personal hostility, I may be permitted to think the reader of your letter curious to know what you would have said if you had happened to have a little personal spite toward the unfortunate object of your invective. If the readers of your letter credit your statements in this regard, I fear, after reading it, they will deem your good-will hate; your kindly feeling toward all men, chronic bitterness; and the best throbbings of your heart, malignity.

I am afraid you do not quite understand your own nature. You will pardon me, therefore, if I hold the mirror up before you for a little while, and let you see yourself as others see you, and thereby convince you how little you have realized the grand old Greek apothegm, "Know thyself."

As one, but not the most remarkable of the examples of your entire ignorance of yourself and the motives which govern your life, I take the astonishing assertion among the closing sentences of your letter: "I have never held public office by my own desire, and certainly wish for none now."

I believe I can show you that you appreciate as little the yearning desire of your heart for office as you do the chronic feeling in your inmost soul of hate and malignity toward me. Let me simply recall certain facts.

You never held a public office by your own desire!!! Why, Judge! you were appointed Judge of the Court of Common Pleas more than a quarter of a century ago, — August 2, 1849, — a very young man for such an office in those times.

You remained on the bench of the Common Pleas until you thought you had got reputation enough from its prestige to enable you to compete with Farley, Wentworth, Abbot, Nelson, and your other associates of the Middlesex bar, so successfully as to earn by your profession larger emoluments than the very moderate salary of an inferior judge, of $2,000 a year; then you resigned the office and tried to earn a living by your profession. Failing in that experiment evidently, because after a short trial at the bar in competing with your peers, when the first opportunity offered, and at your own solicitation, — was it not so, Judge? — you were appointed upon the bench of the Supreme Court, where you served all through the war, sitting on its soft cushions until March 10, 1869, while other men about your own age left their business, quite as lucrative as your salary, and went to the front to do what they could do, to save the country from dismemberment in its hour of peril.

I am bound by candor to say that I never heard any criticism upon your conduct as a judge, save that the infirmity of your temper, the peculiarity of your mind, and the state of your stomach were so unfortunate, that it was said of you by a very distinguished member of the bar, that you were in a continual condition of ill-manners on the bench, both towards your associates, the members of the bar, and the suitors before the court; because you could not gratify the bitterness of your heart, by giving judgment against both parties, in every case.

Indeed with all these infirmities, I am free to say that you made a very passable judge to try small cases, wherein there were no circumstances to excite the Ebenezer of your nature. I am impelled to this observation to demonstrate that I have "no personal hostility" toward Judge Hoar, which might be suspected from the severity of the facts I reluctantly narrate.

Upon the retirement of Chief Justice Bigelow, were you not an applicant for the Chief-Justiceship of that court? and were you not so enraged that Judge Thomas was nominated for that position by Governor Bullock, that you put your resignation of your seat on the bench into the hands of your councillor, Mr. Talbot, to be presented to the council in case Judge Thomas should be confirmed, to show, that should the council confirm Thomas, the State would lose Judge Hoar from the bench; an argument, however, which was a very dangerous one? I am informed, as both your associates of the bench and your brethren at the bar were anxious to be relieved from the burden of bearing your ill-temper and worse manners as a judge, that to get rid of you and get Thomas, both at once, came very near overcoming the political prejudices of the council against confirming him, and I guess would have done it if I had been at the time in full practice before the Supreme Court.

Did not your friends, acting with your knowledge, bring every influence to bear on the council to prevent that confirmation, in which they succeeded? Did not your friends approach by telegraph and otherwise the humble writer of this letter, to advise one of his personal friends, who was a member of the council, to vote against Judge Thomas, and did I not so advise? — not because I doubted his ability as a lawyer, uprightness as a judge, or integrity of life, but because I felt that he was not quite sound on the constitutionality of the legal-tender act, one of the great measures of the war, against which he argued in the case of Parker and Davis, in which I was of counsel. And did not my friend, yielding to such advice as he received from others more capable, as well as myself, vote against Judge Thomas in your favor, giving the determining majority of one on that question? Were you not urged by your friends, with your knowledge and connivance, upon Governor Bullock, for the place of Chief Justice? Now, my dear Judge, as a man accustomed for many years to weigh evidence, does not all this imply on your part, some slight desire for public office? You see that any desire for office, however slight, will convict you of not knowing yourself.

And when fortified by the representations of some of your associates upon the bench, that you were not qualified for the place of Chief Justice, because the infirmities of heart and body of which I have spoken make you liable to take unjust prejudices against one party or the other, in cases where undoubtedly you think yourself unbiased, did not Governor Bullock peremptorily refuse to appoint you, and appoint the late lamented Chief Justice Chapman? As soon as you lost the Chief-Justiceship, were you not, through the recommendation of your representative in Congress, Governor Boutwell, nominated as Attorney-General, another and more lucrative office, upon the first formation of the cabinet of President Grant?

And now, Judge, as to your appointment to the office of Attorney-General of the United States. Is there nothing suggestive of a desire to hold office in that chapter of your political history? Let me recall the facts.

Not being known to President Grant, you were nominated as a member of his first cabinet on a suggestion made by Mr. Boutwell, when the latter gentleman, having declined the position of Secretary of the Interior, tendered to him by the President, was asked to name a suitable person from Massachusetts for the office of Attorney-General? Being thus nominated, you were confirmed by the Senate at an early day, not without surprise on the part of the friends of the administration that you had been selected by the President as one of his constitutional advisers. At the same time Mr. Stewart of New York was nominated Secretary of the Treasury,— a nomination which, failing to be confirmed, was thereafter withdrawn ; leaving that office free to be tendered to Mr. Boutwell, for whom the President had originally intended it, in conformity with the general wish and approval of the Republican party. Now, Judge, what was your conduct toward the President and his administration at that important emergency? Were you not notified authoritatively from the President by a telegram from his most confidential friend, the Hon. Elihu B. Washburn, then Secretary of State, that if you would decline the office of Attorney-General, you would release the administration from embarrassment? You will not deny, Judge, that you received a communication to that effect. And now, in what manner did you respond to the suggestion of the President, thus at the opening of the administration placed in a dilemma for which he was not responsible, having *two* cabinet officers from the same Eastern State? Did you decline the appointment as you were requested to do? By no means. Hastening to Washington without delay, you took the oath of office, thus consummating your official tenure, giving the friends of the administration to understand that you had no thought of retiring, but that you intended "to stick," or perhaps to bring yourself within the terms of the tenure-of-office act. And when it was suggested to you from more than one quarter that you ought to retire from the cabinet in Mr. Boutwell's favor, whom the President desired for his Secretary of the Treasury, especially as you owed your appointment to him, did you not answer in substance, "Let Boutwell go; why should I be asked to?" adding personal ingratitude to the weightier offence of indecorous intrusion into the administration?

Now, Judge, you say that you never held a public office "by your own desire." As, under the circumstances, nobody else desired that you should be Attorney-General at that time, by whose desire were you there? Were not these facts well known and the subject of discussion at the capital?

One who does an ungraceful and ungrateful act to a friend, in order to get in office, ought to desire office very much, in order to excuse his conduct.

You were in office as head of the Department of Justice but eight months when, as the head of that department, it beçame your duty to recommend the appointment of a judge to fill the vacancy that occurred in the Supreme Court. Upon the first occasion, whom did the department send to the President for that place? EBENEZER ROCKWOOD HOAR! If the Department of Justice recommended anybody to the President for that office, Mr. Hoar must have named *himself*. Mr. Stanton, the great War Secretary, was *after*wards nominated, so that you must have preferred yourself as judge to him. But you were rejected by the Senate — but of that more in its proper place.

Do you really think, Judge, upon the whole, that I am uncharitable when I believe that appointment of judge did not rain down on you without some scintilla of a desire to hold public office, or without any procurement, wish expressed, or knowledge on the part of Gen. Grant of that wish, that he should appoint you to a public office for life, out of which you could not be got except you committed an impeachable offence, and bad manners have never been held to be such an one even by myself, who advocated a somewhat broad doctrine as to impeachment? If you insist, however, that I shall believe that the President did appoint you against your desire and will, then I am driven to the other horn of the dilemma,— that he made that appointment without your desire, as an easy and graceful mode of getting you out of his cabinet, which, after your rejection by the Senate, he did do in such a manner that you sent him a very short and curt note of resignation, which did no credit to your good temper or taste.

You may answer, in your own choice language, borrowed from the servant-girls, that he "gave you a character." True,—kind-hearted, good-natured man that he is! — but so he did other cabinet officers, with whose names you would hardly like to have yours coupled.

In a short time, at the next first possible opportunity, we find you holding the office of one of the Commissioners of the United States to settle the treaty as to the "Alabama claims." Did this office also rain down on you without any shadow of desire on your part to hold it? You certainly accepted it with the same alacrity with which you accepted your present bolting nomination for office, at Young's Hotel, being in waiting, as the newspapers tell us, in that building until the committee called you into a meeting which I have reason to know you yourself took part in causing to be organized, to receive your acceptance of a nomination, the letter of which had been before written in Concord, and was in your pocket.

How recklessly you gave up the great fishing interests of Massachusetts, which you were expected to defend and protect, by agreeing to the articles in that treaty which bring all the British Provinces in competition with our own fishermen, and left the United States subject to a reclamation of many millions of dollars by Great Britain on account of those very fisheries, I, in mercy, spare you the recital; besides, I fear a bare statement of the facts about that treaty, in the most courteous language, might, by some uncharitable persons, be construed into "personal abuse."

You are next found holding the office of Presidential Elector, an office with very little to do, indeed, it is true; but then the smallest offices are, by some persons who do not "desire public office," thankfully received.

Once more an office-holder, we find you Representative of the Seventh District. Do you say that you did not want this office? Your son was a delegate to the convention which nominated you, and there are members of that convention who will say, I have been informed, that he actually canvassed in your behalf. Is he so undutiful as to force office on his father against his desire? A bright boy, did he not detect some infinitesimal yearning for office on the part of his parent, and strive to please him by getting it for him?

Next we learn that you made a small run in the Legislature for the office of U. S. Senator from Massachusetts, and were defeated, although the Republican party was largely in the majority. Of course we are to believe that you allowed yourself to be a candidate, and suffer defeat in the candidature for the office, without any desire for the place, precisely as you insist you are running now for an office which you told your friends in the Russell convention, held in the same room at Young's Hotel, that you would not take, if you could get every vote in the district. Now, my dear Judge, don't deny that, because I have it from the gentleman who asked you to be their candidate instead of Russell. Or was your motive in then running for the Senate, as it is now, not to be elected, but simply to defeat the Republican candidate in order to elect a Democrat?

You have your choice of motives.

Either you desired the office and wanted to be elected, or else the same malignity, envy and jealousy which some well-disposed persons believe prompt the present candidature, actuated you then. But much as I have cause to impute bad motives to you, Judge, I prefer to believe it was a desire for the office of Senator which led you to run, because I prefer not to believe that you are actuated by "malice toward all mankind and charity to none;" for, upon the very next vacancy in the Senate, I find you running again for that high office; and I must either believe — the second time certainly — that you desired the office, or believe you hate every Republican and wish to defeat everybody except Democratic candidates.

Another thing, Judge, which is evidence to my mind that you "desired" the office of Senator, is that although the dying Sumner had confided his Civil Rights Bill to your care, when you sat by his death-bedside, — a fact which was telegraphed all over the country by your procurement evidently, as he could not have done it, — yet when you were running for the Senate, J. B. Smith, his life-long friend, then a member of the Legislature, desirous of voting for you, tried in every proper way to get an authorized expression from you in favor of Sumner's bill, which was to be the safeguard of the colored race. He could obtain no expression, and why? A bold stand in favor of the bill would have repelled the Democrats, whom you hoped would come over to you and elect you over your Republican competitors. I should desire public office very much indeed, Judge, before I would seal my lips as to my position on any great measure; but then, you know, Judge, I am only a common erring mortal, and not a "pure-minded," cold-blooded, unselfish statesman, *who has spent half his life in office not "by his own desire."*

I wish to do you justice. I admit that you might have been elected to the present Congress instead of Mr. Tarbox or Dr. Ayer, and refused the office when you might have had it. I am bound to say thus much, because it is the first office I ever knew you to refuse. Still, you will remember, my dear Judge, you told me the reason was that you could not afford to take it; that a man could only live in Washington respectably on the salary; and yet, my dear Judge, one of your objections to me in your letter is what you are pleased to call a "salary grab," which means, I suppose, that I voted for an increase of that inadequate salary which has deprived the present Congress of your great talents.

When you say "salary grab," you certainly could not refer to the fact that I took what is called "back pay," — that is, pay received for services for a time previous to its being voted — service rendered under a contract, as it is claimed — to work for a smaller salary, because when you were Judge of the Supreme Court in 1866 your pay was raised from three thousand to four thousand dollars a year, and you took the "back pay" which the Legislature voted you, with the same alacrity that you have always run for and taken office without any "desire" for it. True, you may say that your back pay was not a large amount; but then, if it is a "salary grab" to take "back pay," you fell with much slighter temptation than I did, for the amount which came to me was considerably larger. Now don't misunderstand me, Judge. I do not think it was wrong for you to take that "back pay;" but, having taken it, it does not seem good taste to make railing accusations against me for doing the same thing, because yours was "such a little one." Such a procedure does not seem the emanation of a judicial mind.

The last public office — for I think it is a high and honorable one — which you held was that of Delegate to the Cincinnati Convention for the selection of a presidential candidate for the Republican party. True, you might not have desired that office, although you accepted, because there *was no pay* attached to it except what seems to me the highest compensation for public service, — an opportunity to do good to the country.

To use a mode of statement copied from your letter, "as the newspapers inform us," — by which one can make an injurious imputation without making himself responsible for it, an ingenious device, which does credit to your cunning but not to your courage, — not wanting the office, you got elected to it by representing yourself, or being represented, as an advocate of the candidature of Mr. Blaine; and, "as the newspapers inform us," when you got to Cincinnati you turned up something very different entirely; not a friend of Governor Hayes, for whom you now express admiration, because you so managed yourself and your colleagues that you not only contrived to cover yourself and the State with merited ridicule, but also never cast its vote for Governor Hayes; for, with a perversity of political senselessness which I always, in you, attribute to bad health, or bad temper, or both, you kept the vote of the Massachusetts delegation on other candidates, so that owing to your management Massachusetts in the convention never cast her vote for Hayes at all. He was nominated without her aid, and you now seem to be managing the Republican party of Massachusetts in the best manner, if it were possible so to do, to have Hayes elected without her vote. I hope and believe you may not so divide and distract the party as to be successful in what seems to be your aim, — its destruction only.

Now, my dear Judge, let us count up. You have been appointed to four different offices, and elected to three. Your services in them, covering by far the largest part of your business life, were in the appointive offices, being of the class of the largest emolument, and the three elective offices having but little or no emolument, for I do not think a representative in Congress has any. You have been appointed to, candidate for, and voted for, and failed to get six of the highest offices in the gift of the appointing power or of the Commonwealth, which if you had got would have occupied the whole of the rest of your lifetime, and are now running for another, with about the same show of success that you had of being Chief Justice of the Commonwealth, or a Justice of the Supreme Court of the United States.

In view of these facts, which I have been compelled to set out with a tediousness in length, — for which I owe you, who have to read this letter, an apology, which is, if you had not held so many offices, and been candidate for so many more, I could have made it shorter, — do you, my dear Judge, really think I add the suspiciousness of unbelief to my other short-comings which you have enumerated, when I say I cannot believe you when you say "I never held public office by my own desire"? To others the inveteracy of your office-holding seems only equalled by the continuity of your office-seeking: both are chronic and have been the business, not the episodes, of your life.

Let us tabulate your want of "desire" for public office: —

TABLE OF OFFICES HELD, APPLIED FOR, RUN FOR AND LOST BY HON. E. R. HOAR, WITHOUT ANY DESIRE FOR ANY OF THEM.

Appointed.	Elected.	Candidate for and lost.
Judge of Common Pleas. Judge of Supreme Court. Attorney General. Commissioner on Alabama Claims.	Member of Congress. Presidential Elector. Delegate to Convention.	Chief Justice Supreme Court, Mass. Judge of Supreme Court of United States. Senator in place of Sumner. Senator in place of Wilson. Member of Congress (bolted to get it).
Total 4	Total 3	Total 5

Grand total 12

I have no doubt that you believed yourself when you wrote that "you had never held public office by your own desire;" but then, as I told you to begin with, you don't know yourself or see yourself as others see you.

I doubt not you as firmly believe that you "have no personal hostility to me" as you do that you "never held public office by your own desire." The trouble seems to be that you have got the cardinal virtues and the deadly sins so mixed up in your mind that you mistake greed for office for public virtue, covetousness for generosity, hate for love, malice for good will, prejudices for convictions, dyspepsia for a conscience, and cultivate malignity as a parlor plant, believing it to be one of the Christian graces. Indeed, your state of feeling toward me seems formulated by Tennyson's lines, wherein he describes the kind of love his heroine bore to her lover who had betrayed her sister: —

"I hated him with the hate of hell,
But I loved his beauty passing well."

Not to compare small things with great, let me, in a word, give you my own record as a public officer. I have never held office or received a dollar of public money for pay as an officer, save as a soldier in the service, or as a legislator. But I held both these positions by "my own desire," and sought them to gratify an honorable ambition, and to be of service to my country. I leave it to the just judgment of all men which has been the "office-jobber."

Having exhibited to you as well as I may the condition of your mental and moral organism at the moment you wrote your letter, "to supply the ripe wants of a friend," I break a custom and reply to some of its statements. As long as they are simply the emanations of newspaper slang-whangers, I make it the rule of my life to live down slanders, not to reply to them. But coming from so respectable a source, it is due to yourself to set you right about many things in regard to myself, where you are clearly wrong, as your statements, distorted by the medium of a perverse imagination, clouded by a deep-seated feeling of revenge for fancied wrongs, make evident.

You say that "at the last State convention at which he [myself] sought the nomination for Governor, and led his own forces, it was only after they had been detected in a large amount of double voting, that he yielded to the will of the honest majority. It was on that occasion that he asked, with a humor of his own, why it was always insisted on taking extraordinary precautions to secure an honest vote whenever he happened to be a candidate."

You will pardon me, Judge, for saying that I never used that expression, and no reported proceedings of the convention made at the time will so show. You say "they were never needed in a Republican State convention in Massachusetts before." You are mistaken, Judge. The record of the ballot taken for Lieutenant-Governor, when I was not a candidate, showed a vote largely in excess of the true one. Ask Gov. Talbot how he was treated. At this very convention of which you speak, *I am prepared to show that I was cheated out of the nomination.* Up to this hour I have steadily declined to make the charge or produce the evidence. I have covered it as did the sons of Noah the disgrace of their father, when they walked backwards and threw over him their cloaks to conceal the sin of the old man. In the first place, at nearly twelve o'clock at night, more votes were thrown after hundreds of the delegates had gone home, than the entire number which could properly be members of the convention if all were present. And no unprejudiced man can believe that such a vote could possibly be thrown at that hour of the night. The opposition, led by a political priest, a kind of man that all history shows is the most unscrupulous and dangerous of all men in political affairs, was organized on the cry "ANYTHING TO BEAT BUTLER."

Who were the unauthorized voters who carried that convention at Worcester against me at midnight? I have the evidence, and can exhibit it in the shape of sworn testimony when called for by the party organization. If the Republican party desire that I shall go farther into the investigation, and produce the evidence to its disgrace, unwilling as I am to blot the record of the party, I will do it. But I state the fact to be, sustained by sworn evidence, that, at midnight, after many members of the convention had given up their tickets and left to take the cars for their homes, as they declared, in reply to the inquiry of the door-keeper if they wished to return to the convention, the Chairman of the Committee on Tickets, under whose instruction the door-keeper was acting, came to him and took a package of tickets from him, and went downstairs with them; that immediately thereupon a large number of new delegates appeared, passing in on the strength of those tickets. This Chairman of the Committee was an anti-Butler man, by *genus*, and of the Hoar *species*, and of course acting against me. I know him and his name, and whenever he chooses to deny the fact he will be very efficiently answered. Whether correctly or not, I firmly believed at that time that I was disgracefully jockeyed out of that nomination by you and your associates; but I refused to bolt the nomination, lest that bolt should affect the integrity of the party, and for no other reason whatever. In other words, I did what I doubt you, from your mental constitution, are capable of doing, — I sacrificed my personal feelings for the good of the party and the country.

A word in your ear privately, Judge: the less you say about that convention the better.

Again: You say that "when he boasted to two of his colleagues in Washington in 1874, that he got *their* telegrams before they did; that *he had a man* who read them off the wires by the click." I deny that I made any such boast. Let any two of my colleagues come forward and say that I used those words to them. I knew of but *one man* who was telegraphing from Washington to Boston upon the occasion you speak of, and therefore I could not have said it. Second: I never said "I *had a man*" who read the telegrams from the wires by the click.

When a foolish contest was raised over the confirmation of the Collector of the Port of Boston, the whole country became interested in the fight, and information poured in to me from all quarters. Do you mean to say that you would not have received such information? The very next sentence of your letter convicts you. You say, "And if, *as the newspapers inform us*, he employed such an agent as John D. Sanborn to dog the steps of Mr. Peirce in New York, and find out his business there, General Butler showed that he regarded as legitimate weapons of political warfare, means which in private or professional life he would undoubtedly think base and dishonorable."

"And if, as the newspapers inform us," where did you and the newspapers get that information? From a telegraphic dispatch of mine, filched from a committee-room by a dishonest subordinate, for I won't believe that even a committee of a Confederate Congress would permit the publication of private dispatches of private individuals. And you make use of that information derived from that telegram, so stolen and published, to make a charge against me. You say the use of information derived from the telegram of another, in your own choice language, is "on a level with listening at key-holes or picking pockets;" yet in this very letter you have done that very thing, and shelter yourself under, "And if, as the newspapers inform us." Speak up like a man now, Judge, and say whether you did not know that the information you use was from one of my own private telegrams, and no other source whatever.

I have no cause to be ashamed or disturbed at the publication of that telegram, or in stating exactly what I did. The Simmons fight was over. I had been informed that Mr. Henry L. Peirce had gone to New York to get a New York man to apply for the position of minister at Venezuela, as against the present minister, a distinguished citizen of Massachusetts, whom I favored; Peirce hoping, as the Secretary of State was from New York, he might break my recommendation with the State department by producing a New Yorker as a candidate for the place. Wishing to ascertain if the information I had received was true, I sent to a constituent of mine, Mr. John D. Sanborn, whom I knew to be in New York, to ascertain the facts, and who Peirce's candidate was to be, if he had one, so that I might put the Secretary of State on his guard. Is there anything illegitimate or improper in so doing? Yet you indulge in a spiteful fling at a man in these words: "He employed such an agent as John D. Sanborn." Now, Judge, Mr. Sanborn is your equal in everything that makes an honest man, and your superior in many things which make up a good member of society, and I know you both very well. Through your machinations, and those of another member of the delegation whose name I will not now mention, — for I am waiting for him to take a hand in this fight, as it is my custom not to be the aggressor, — an investigation for weeks was had of Mr. Sanborn, particularly because it was supposed that through that investigation you could get at me. The Committee of Ways and Means found that Mr. Sanborn had done nothing that the law did not direct and authorize him to do; and if there was any fault in what he had done, it was a fault of the law. A majority of the Republican members of that committee recommended the Commissioners of Internal Revenue to again employ him in the collection of delinquent taxes; and he has been employed from that day to this more or less in that work, under Mr. Bristow, for whom you voted as candidate for President, as against Governor Hayes, and that, too, without any recommendation or interference on my part.

Your malice toward me seems to make you unjust to everybody else, for you say, "Collectors detail subordinates to attend to his errands and run his campaign." Now, if you did not know that to be true, Judge, then you told what you did not know to be true, as if it were true; and that you will recognize yourself as being the most vicious kind of falsification. No collector, past or present, has ever detailed any man to attend to my errands or run any of my campaigns. Men do kindly things for me from motives which you cannot possibly appreciate and can hardly understand, because you never did a service to any man without pay down that I ever heard of; therefore, you never knew what it was to have men grateful enough to you, and kindly enough disposed towards you to, of their own free will and friendliness, do everything they can do for you. I would advise you to try to act kindly towards somebody once, and get somebody to feel in that way towards yourself once. It would be a new sensation, and would please you with its novelty, if it did not touch your heart.

In your kindly manner, you speak of me as one "whom the voters of the Sixth District could tolerate no longer," meaning, I suppose, that I was defeated in the Sixth District in my last candidature. Would you not think it personal abuse if I should say of you that you were not fit to run for Congress, because in your last two Senatorial candidatures you were ignominiously beaten, and that, therefore, the people of the Commonwealth never would "tolerate" you at all? Or would you think I was dealing kindly with your brother, George F. Hoar, if I taunted him with the words, "The people of Worcester will not 'tolerate' you, because in the same campaign of 1874 in which I was defeated he lost a greater number of votes than I did of his former Republican majority in the heart of the Commonwealth, and was only elected by 462 votes, when he had a plurality the election before of 7,684 votes? this great loss, in my judgment, being in part caused by the unjust acts of yourself and your associates towards myself in the gubernatorial convention. He yielded, however, to what he seems to have regarded as the popular verdict, and has not dared since to try the result of an election by the people in any district.

Your next objection is expressed in these words: "Gen. Butler was in favor of paying the national debt in greenbacks, — a measure which the Republican party has thought inconsistent with the national honor, — and has recently avowed his belief that the policy of *providing for a speedy return to specie payments* is unsound, oppressive and mischievous."

One would have supposed that a man who has been accustomed to charge juries upon facts would state an opponent's position with more accuracy. I never was in favor of paying the "national debt" in greenbacks. The larger part of it could not be so paid. I said, what you do not dare to deny as a lawyer, that the contract, under which the five-twenty bonds were issued in 1862, was that they should be paid in greenbacks; and no respectable member of the bar, who has ever examined the question, has come to a different opinion, — but they were but a small part of the national debt.

Again: I never have "avowed my belief that the *policy of providing* for a speedy return to specie payments is unsound." My proposition has always been, and you will find it in my letter of acceptance, that what I have objected to is the policy of *attempting* by law to return to specie payments *without providing the means* by which our currency might be raised to specie values, and thus make specie payments possible. In case of some men I should be charitable enough to suppose that they did not see the difference between the two statements; but you, Judge, I know to have a too discriminating mind in dealing with propositions not to understand the exact difference; and your looseness of statement of my position shows that you dare not go to the people with an accurate statement of it. Having, many times over, and in my letter of acceptance of the candidature, said that my difficulty was that I thought it impossible to return to specie payments by legal enactment alone; that such a course would be oppressive to the debtor; and that I thought it far better that the country should so grow in credit so that provision might be made for a return to specie values, but that, as the party had resolved to the contrary, and the Democratic party had apparently come on the same platform, the experiment would have to be tried, — I am quite willing you should make all out of that objection to me you can; but please don't delude anybody by a garbled statement of my position.

Again: You are pleased to say that the convention which nominated me, although composed of delegates elected by the Republicans in the several towns at meetings called for that purpose, and at one of which you yourself presided, according to the exact usage of the Republican party, if it does not nominate to suit you, "becomes a bolting convention." Be it so. Then why not have the State Committee or the District Committee call another? Where did you get your credentials to call one at Young's Hotel? If you will call another convention, Judge, in the Seventh District, of the voters, through the regular party organization, and promise not to bolt if you lose, I will resubmit my nomination to that convention, and you yourself may run as a candidate. I promise to abide by the result.

You say that the convention which nominated me "was not the entertainment to which you were invited;" but this is an entertainment to which you are invited. I will even contest Concord with you, for a delegation, provided you won't hold the hat at the caucus in which the votes are deposited, as you did at the last one.

If you are right that the late convention in the Seventh District was a bolting convention only, there would seem to be a necessity for the call of another, because that convention nominated an elector for President and Vice-President of the United States, for the Republican votes of the district, and there certainly ought to be a regular nomination by the Republican party for Elector for President, and there is none now if that convention was a "bolting convention."

Again: At the State convention the delegates from my district put me in nomination before that convention as a member of the State Central Committee. That would have been a good opportunity for you to have contested my status in the Republican party. The State convention would surely have a right to reject the nomination of any man on the State Central Committee who was not a Republican; but you thought it, doubtless, easier to get a vote on my republicanism in a convention of your thirty-five friends at Young's Hotel, than in the State convention, composed of Republican delegates. I will try that question with you, Judge, in any State convention where you will agree that the chairman of the Committee on Tickets won't take packages of tickets, deposited with the door-keeper by delegates that have gone home, out and distribute them among your friends to come in and vote as delegates of the convention. Without precaution against such "methods" as that, I am willing to admit I should again be beaten; because those are not the " methods " that I employ.

Your next objection is, that I am " a scoffer of civil-service reform." No, Judge, you mistake; I am only a scoffer at hypocrisy. If I understand civil-service reform, it means, members of Congress shall not interfere with the executive departments in the selection of their subordinates, by which those departments are to be carried on. Am I right in that as a part of the scheme of civil-service reform? Very well: let me state a fact, Judge, which illustrates the difference between preaching and practice.

When the Secretary of the Treasury directed the cutting down of the expenses of the Boston Custom House some $40,000, by the dismissal, among other things, of useless officers, I never interfered or advised in the selection of the officers that were to be dismissed, nor did I ask to have any friend or supporter of mine retained. I assumed that the Collector would know what was for the benefit of the public service in that regard, and I did not know. Now, Judge, let me ask you two or three questions.

In the process of that reduction did not the Collector relieve from duty two officers from the Seventh District, appointed with your recommendation as its representative in Congress, discharged as a part of the necessary reduction of his force?

Was he not called to Washington thereupon by Secretary Bristow, and did he not meet you, then a member of Congress, before the Secretary? Did you not then insist to the Secretary that the Collector should restore those men, and argue at length that your men should be retained in office, although the Collector had certified to the Secretary that their services were no longer needed, nor the services of anybody else in their places? Did not the Collector in your presence state to you that these men's services were not required, and did you not still insist that they should be kept because they were your appointees?

When, in the course of your speech to the Secretary, you referred to my district, did not the Collector call your attention to the fact that I had not interfered with his action in behalf of any of the Custom House employés in my district, but had left him to do according to the dictates of his own judgment, and that yourself and brother, who, I think, was present, were the only two members of Congress who had ever interfered with him as to which of his subordinates he should discharge? Yielding to your importun.ties, pressed with great vehemence, did not the Secretary finally order these men — good men, I doubt not, but not needed — to be retained, and did not the Collector obey that order? And were not two men thus fastened upon the Treasury by you, a member of Congress, that were not needed, in opposition to the judgment of the officer charged with the carrying on of that branch of the public service?

That, Judge, is the kind of civil-service reform I scoff at; and nothing but my personal respect for you, and the entire absence of "personal hostility" toward me on your part, prevents my scoffing at the reformer!

Now, Judge, how, after that, could you go to Cincinnati and vote for civil-service reform? or were you, in that regard, as well as in regard to the candidature of Mr. Blaine, one thing in Massachusetts and another in Cincinnati? "Thou hypocrite, first cast out the beam out of thine own eye, and then thou shalt see clearly to cast out the mote out of thy brother's eye."

The difference between us, Judge, is this, as I understand it: I do full as well as I preach; you preach a great deal better than you do.

Your next objection I find to be that "the nomination of General Butler in this district by a Republican convention, and the placing him on the State Republican Committee by the delegates of Lowell, is doing our party incalculable harm throughout the country."

Where do you find the evidence of that, Judge? I have had invitations to speak during the campaign from twenty odd political organizations in the States in the North, and four in the South. In this campaign I have been obliged to refuse in every instance but one. Called by public business to the State of Ohio, I spoke there at the most earnest request of the Republican organization of the county. After that I received the most urgent appeals from the Republican organization of the State of Indiana to go there; but I learned while in Ohio of the initiation of your Young's Hotel cabal against the integrity of the Republican party in Massachusetts, and I refused to go to Indiana, as I had before refused, and published my refusal. And while I don't claim that I could have done much good by taking part in the canvass, yet I will state a fact or two.

Your letter dates your objections to me as a Republican as far back as 1867; and what I have done has not been done in a corner.

You will hardly claim that I am any different now, either for better or worse, than in 1872, when, at the request of the National and State Committees, I canvassed almost the entire States of Maine and Indiana, and a large portion of New York, a portion of Illinois and Ohio, for the Republican nominees for President and Vice-President, travelling some 3,000 miles and making sixty speeches. Indiana was then carried by an overwhelming majority; and from the earnest appeals of its Republican organization, and of Senator Morton and others to me, to come there again this year, I infer that they thought my "methods" of canvass had done, and would do, good. Mischievous interference with the politics of the Seventh District has kept me out of Indiana this year, and it has gone Democratic. If you will look at the returns in the precinct where I spoke in Ohio you will find that it quite maintained its majority of last year. Now I don't say *propter hoc*, but I have a right to say *post hoc*. I had rather take the opinion of the true, fighting, earnest Republicans of Indiana and Ohio who did not vote for nor elect Democratic Congressmen two years ago, upon the question of the value of my services to the Republican party, than that of yourself or your associates, who sent a Democrat to Congress from the Republican State of Massachusetts by your votes.

Whenever the Republican party can say to me, "Gen. Butler, you have wilfully, by your influence and votes directly used for that purpose, caused the return of Democratic members of Congress," I, in common decency, shall withdraw myself from that party, and shall certainly not attempt to dictate to its voters their nominees; nor shall I have the hardihood to present myself for their suffrages on the ground that I am a better Republican than any one who for sixteen years has done all in his power for its success.

I have again to complain, Judge, of your attempt in your letter to so word it as not to make charges for which I can hold you responsible, but simply to make a statement in such manner as to leave the charge to be inferred. I quote as follows: —

"What, but the deep-seated and wide-spread dissatisfaction excited at the North at the Sanborn moieties, salary-grabs, the bargains, contracts, office-jobbing and caucus-packing, which occur to every man's mind when Gen. Butler's name is mentioned in connection with politics?"

Thus you mean to leave it to be inferred that I had something to do with the "Sanborn moieties." You know—and therefore you ought not to have made such a statement—that, whether the "Sanborn moieties" were right or wrong, I had nothing to do with them whatever. I neither advised his employment, recommended him, or did anything about them, directly or indirectly. Months of investigation, inspired by you and one of your colleagues, demonstrated that fact, as it now stands upon record. Whether the "Sanborn moieties" were right or wrong depended upon the law which authorized them, which did not emanate from any committee of which I was a member, and with which I had nothing to do, and with the administration of which law I never interfered or took part.

Under a law passed by Congress after debate, Mr. Sanborn was employed to collect taxes from railroads that had cheated the government out of them and withheld them for more than five years. The law gave him half for making the collections and discovering the frauds, and for that I had no responsibility; and he was not employed to do the business until two other parties had been employed and failed to make the collections. But I will now say that, in my belief, more than $5,000,000 of withheld taxes have been lost to the United States because of the raid upon that law instituted in part by yourself in the hope of striking at me.

"Bargains" did you say, Judge? Why, I never made but one political bargain of sufficient consequence to be in my memory for a day, save with you and your free-soil friends, in 1849–50, by which the Democrats were to give the free-soilers the Senator, in case of success, and you were to give us the State Government. That bargain was fairly carried out, was called the "coalition," and elected Sumner; and we thought it all right and "pure," didn't we, Judge? But, bless us! Judge B. R. Curtis published a pamphlet, in which he gave it as his deliberate legal opinion that our "*bargain*" *or* "*coalition*" *was an indictable conspiracy at common law*. How differently different people look upon the acts even of as "pure" a man as yourself, to be sure! That ought to teach you, Judge, to have a little charity and leniency in your judgment of poor me.

In the matter of "contracts," I have never had or made any contract with the government, nor have had any interest in any except as a member of a Company which has done work for the government, precisely the same as any other individual in the community.

"Contracts" in relation to government matters, do I hear you say, Judge? Well, I will tell you what I think would be a contract about government affairs which would be disgraceful for me to enter into; and I think you will agree with me. If I should be employed by the government, or anybody else, to give a legal opinion upon and manage a law case, and, after I had done so, and become conversant with all the points on that side, I should take employment on the other side, and receive large fees for my services, specially because of my knowledge of the case, got when I was the lawyer for the first party, I should say I had disgraced myself, my profession and my State; and I am certain if I had done so you would have mentioned it in your letter as a reason why you could not support me for Congress.

Well, then, Judge (correct me if I get the facts wrong — and I shall not need correction), did not the Central Pacific Railroad have a claim for many millions of land grant and bonds, to be given by the United States as a subsidy, depending upon certain law points, and also upon the approval of a map of location, which was so preposterous that even Andrew Johnson would not approve it, as it would take many millions out of the Treasury without any equivalent?

Were not these law questions pending before the Department of Justice, having been reported to it before you became Attorney-General? Did you not hear, or read printed arguments upon them, while acting for the United States as its Attorney-General?

Did not those arguments fail to convince you that you ought to advise the President to approve that map, and you did not so advise him? Was not that all so?

You did right, Judge; nobody had bribed you or offered to bribe you to give a different opinion that I know of.

Immediately after you resigned your office of Attorney-General, did you not receive a large retainer (*not too large for such a service*) on behalf of the Central Pacific Railroad, to argue this very case of theirs before the Executive or other departments of the government? And did you not so argue?

Nay, did you not, under the pressure of your fees, go to the President and use all possible political, personal and legal influence upon him, as his late law adviser, to prevail upon the President to approve that map and thereby lay the foundation for filching out of the people of the United States, in land and bonds, quite as many millions as you are years old? Do you yourself believe that you received your retainers on your supposed merits as a lawyer, or simply because of the knowledge obtained and influence acquired by you in the case—because you had been Attorney-General? Of course the railroad got you *as ex-Attorney-General*, not as lawyer. If the latter had been what they paid for, they would have retained you before, as you were a better lawyer before you were Attorney-General than after. My dear Judge, getting into high office seems to have shrivelled you up as a lawyer somehow, as a ripe pear is sometimes by too much light in the fall; at least I thought so when we tried the Weld case together, when you let your clients in for a $400,000 judgment.

I am making this letter too long, Judge, so that I will not say anything *now* about the other retainers you took against the government in other railroads and the wool case, where you not only argued what the law was, but testified what you, as legislator, enacted it to be, and so the government lost *three-quarters of a million.*

My quiver is by no means exhausted. I am keeping a few arrows for the next fight.

As to office-jobbing, by which, if I understand, you mean selling offices, I never received, directly or indirectly, one penny for putting any man in or out of office. Nor have I ever known but a single officer of my recommendation fail in his duty to the government, and as soon as I had knowledge of that failure I recommended his removal.

The next charge which you leave to be inferred against me is "caucus-packing." I hardly know that I precisely understand what you mean by that. If you mean that when I have been a candidate for elective office I have wished my friends to attend the caucus in my behalf, I have done that, and no more; and you, I am certain, have done the same. First, because at that State Convention where you appeared to oppose me, I am informed that you were elected a delegate at a caucus in Concord where there were but seven individuals present, and four of them your relatives by blood or marriage. I never packed or unpacked a caucus so badly as that in my life. Again, at the last caucus in Concord to nominate delegates to the Seventh District Convention, the action of which you bolt, when you presided, fearing that there were not enough of your friends present to carry the caucus, delayed the proceedings until your son and your retainers scoured the streets of Concord and hauled men into the caucus, and were enabled by so doing to get twelve majority, out of one hundred and eight voters, against me, you yourself holding the hat into which the ballots were deposited; so that I am told some men on whom you had influence or other claims did not vote as they had previously declared they would do. But of this I speak of information and belief, and not of personal knowledge.

I believe now I have examined every charge you bring against me in your letter. I have opposed to every one that affects my personal character my denial, and I challenge the proof in a single instance to invalidate that denial. You yourself have been careful to so word the charges that I cannot hold you responsible for either of them in any forum where the questions can be tested by evidence. Make any charge reflecting on my character as an honest man and a good citizen, directly, and you will have an opportunity to make good that charge before some tribunal that can take jurisdiction over it.

Your dislike, to give it no harsher name, toward me will incite you to destroy a political rival who, you think, — but there you are wrong, — defeated your nomination before the United States Senate. I want to assure you now, in this public manner, — and any Senator that knows to the contrary will inform you if I am wrong, — that in that contest I took no part. I deemed you unfit for a Judge of the Supreme Court of the United States for reasons of fitness not affecting your personal integrity, but for reasons of the same nature as would prevent my putting a balky horse in a team, even if he were well blooded. I did not interfere, however, with your confirmation, because everybody in Washington knew that you did not stand a ghost of a chance of being confirmed. You had been there just long enough for people to know you, and the Senate of the United States is too august a body to be affected in their action by the personal *clacque* of a mutual-admiration society in Massachusetts. Therefore you were rejected, with but twelve Senators, as I am informed, of either party, voting in your favor, after most strenuous efforts in your behalf by the two Senators from Massachusetts, with the added prestige of a nomination by President Grant, then in the zenith of his power and influence. I don't remember now of a single other instance where the nomination of an Associate Justice of the Supreme Court of the United States has been rejected when the majority of the Senate was in political accord with the President. Therefore I infer that there must have been some radical defect as to your personal fitness which caused the catastrophe. I doubt if you fully comprehend what the matter was yourself; because, as I have already told you, you don't see yourself as others see you.

Now, Judge, you and I have lived in the County of Middlesex *forty-eight years* together; you have known of my incomings and outgoings; you are a lawyer of ability; you know the power of evidence. If you know of any act of mine which affects my personal integrity, or believe you can prove one, state it over your name specifically, "I know or can prove this or that;" and if you do prove it, you will destroy me and gratify your spleen.

Having thus disposed of your political charges against me, I come to what ought, in my judgment, to affect your candidature for any office in the minds of all just men. "Caucus-packing" may be very bad, if by it you understand bringing men into a caucus to carry a political point against fair and honest judgment. Be it so; but how does that compare in enormity with packing the bench of the Supreme Court of the United States in order to reverse a fair and honest judgment upon a great question of constitutional law and right, and involving the interests of every man in the country? Of this political wickedness, Judge, you are guilty, and I now submit the proof. My allegations, you see, are specific, direct, positive; and I am responsible for them.

The facts are as follows:—

As we have seen, you were Attorney-General, at the head of the Department of Justice of the United States, in 1869. The case of *Hepburn* vs. *Griswold*, involving the constitutionality of the legal-tender act, had been and was before the Supreme Court for its final determination in November of that year. On the 27th day of which month the Court came to a conclusion, by a majority of five to three, Chief Justice Chase presiding, that the legal-tender act, even as a war measure, in its action in time of peace, was beyond the constitutional power of Congress. Upon the recommendation of the Department of Justice, of which you were the chief, Congress had passed an act (April 10, 1869), to take effect on the first Monday of December, that there should be appointed an additional judge. The Court had postponed the announcement of their decision of November 27, 1869, as to the constitutionality of the legal-tender act until the seventh day of February, 1870, in order to give time to write up their opinions.

It was the duty of the Attorney-General, as head of the Department of Justice, to advise the President as to the appointment of judges of the Supreme Court. The President was so advised that *you*, YOURSELF, the ATTORNEY-GENERAL, were nominated on the 14th of December, 1869, to that seat so created. You had already made a decision in favor of the constitutionality of the legal-tender act in what was known as the "*Essex Company Cases*," when on the bench of Massachusetts, as well as in the case of *Davis and Parker*.

On the day after you were nominated — to wit, the 15th day of December — Judge Grier resigned his seat on the Supreme Bench, to take effect on the 1st day of February, 1870. On the 20th day of December, the President, on the recommendation, it is to be presumed, of the Department of Justice, nominated Secretary Stanton to the vacancy to be created by the resignation of Mr. Justice Grier. Secretary Stanton's views on the question of the constitutionality of the legal-tender act were as well known as your own; but, to the grief of all, he died some four days after his nomination. Meanwhile the decision of the Supreme Court on the constitutionality of the legal-tender act had become known, and was commented on in the public press, — the opinion of Mr. Justice Grier having been directed by the Court to be read on the 29th of January, before his resignation took effect on the 1st of February. On the third day of February, your nomination, as I have before stated, was quite unanimously rejected by the Senate. If Stanton had lived and you had been confirmed, then you would thus have added two judges to the bench to make a majority to reverse the decision against the constitutionality of the legal-tender act. You know, without my telling you, how much your conduct in regard to this decision of the Court affected the judgment of the Judiciary Committee of the Senate upon your case. The opinions of the Court were read on the 7th day of February. On the 8th day of February, it appears by the record of the Senate, being cabinet day, you advised the nomination of two judges who had already formed and given legal opinions in favor of the constitutionality of the legal-tender act. It was not the fault of these gentlemen that they were thus put upon the Court to make a given decision, because they knew nothing of the purpose; but, by your action, the majority of the Court was changed so that they would stand five to four upon that question, as they afterwards, upon a reargument of it, did stand. You had tried to call up the original case for reargument and reconsideration, but failed. Having thus packed the Court on your side of the question, you applied to the Court to bring forward two other cases for argument, which application was granted, so that the question whether greenbacks were money was brought before a Court to which you had added two judges who had formed and expressed an opinion favorable to your side of the case. What would you say of me, if in one of my cases I had used official power to put jurors on the panel whom I knew had formed and expressed an opinion in favor of my client's case? Is it any better because the Attorney-General does the same thing in behalf of the government? The jurors would not be to blame if they did not know why they were put on the jury, as did not the judges in this case. I do not speak of the decision, whether right or wrong. Of course, the decision was your way. By your action, and yours alone, as the head of the Department of Justice, in advising the President, the Court was packed with a majority of judges to determine one way a great constitutional question and reverse a solemn decision already made.

You now claim to be in favor of the immediate resumption of specie payments. If you had let the first decision of the Court stand, and not taken this extraordinary means to reverse it, which you did, the country would have returned to specie payments then and there, because we should have had no other constitutional money, the greenback having been declared no longer to be money, or legal tender for debts, and we should have had no money but gold and silver. You think such a return to specie payments desirable. *To that you alone were the obstructionist.* It is your action alone which prevented a resumption of specie payments more than *six years ago*, which you think now so vital, "affecting the industry, the wages, the property, the prosperity of every member of the community." I quote from your letter. Why, then, did you not let the resumption of specie payments alone when it had come by the action of the Supreme Court of the United States?

If the resumption of specie payments will do all you claim for it, what mischief you have done by preventing it, and how? By packing, with judges whom you knew would decide the question in your favor, the Supreme Court of the United States, — an act of political corruption, and fraught with dangers greater than any other which has ever occurred in the history of the nation.

Following your teaching, what shall prevent the Democratic party, if they can get in power, from creating additional judgeships, to which the judges can be appointed by President Tilden, confirmed by the Senate, who will make a majority of the Court, to decide that every act of the government by which the rebellion was suppressed, by which the rebel debt was repudiated, and by which payment for slaves was inhibited, are unconstitutional and void? You taught the Democratic party that lesson. You set them the example. You shew them that trick, and I doubt not they will profit by your teaching and your example.

Judge Hoar, if I ever do anything so terribly mischievous to the institutions of my country as this, I will hide my head in shame, and never again let it be seen among men, lest I should be pointed at as one who has polluted the courts of justice in the highest Court of his country.

I wish, for your sake, and the sake of Massachusetts, I could stop here; but justice requires still further illumination of your record. Having done what you had done, and resorted to the demoralizing proceeding you had to secure a judgment of the Supreme Court of the United States in favor of the constitutionality of the legal-tender act, and to have the greenback sustained as the true and constitutional money, and to prevent an immediate resumption of specie payments, — you were elected as a representative to Congress from the Seventh District, and there in your place made a motion that the resumption of specie payments should take place on the first day of September, 1874, or in less than five months, which motion, when amended to the fourth day of July, 1876, hardly obtained twenty votes in a house composed of a two-thirds majority of your party friends. But, wonderful to relate! in advocating that motion, you made an argument that greenbacks were not *money*, — the very greenback money which you had caused to be decided to be money and legal tender, even by debauching the course of justice in the highest court of the land.

I give your words from the Congressional Record: —

" VOL. 2, PART 3, 43D CONGRESS.

" April 9, 1874.

have no time or inclination to discuss with any gentleman the question whether whatever the government chooses to call money is money; whether by putting a government stamp upon a piece of paper you can make it money. I believe that you might just as well say that you make a man an honest or sensible man by giving him a certificate that he is elected to Congress."

Can political tergiversation, — can corruption in " method of political procedure," — can tampering with the judiciary of the country, — can playing, as if with dice, with great interests and great constitutional questions, — can undermining and sapping the very foundations of all our liberties and rights by interference with the course of justice in the Supreme Court — further go?

I grieve that I am obliged to make these disclosures. I would I were permitted to draw a veil over them and blot them out from the record forever; but it is impossible. They stand there written in letters of light for the condemnation of every true, patriotic and right-thinking man.

I submit this record of yours to the judgment of the people and of your peers in the profession of the law. I submit it to the learned judges, your brothers upon the bench in the several courts of the Union, and ask, with all the solemnity the gravity of the act demands, what ought to be done to the man who has thus pulled down the main pillar which supports the fabric of the government, the trust and credit which all men ought to give to the decisions of the highest judicial tribunal of the United States?

My sense of right and propriety of conduct may not be too keen. Of that others must judge. But I thank God I can go to my pillow, as I am about doing, as I finish this communication to you, without the stain of such an act upon my conscience.

I have the honor to subscribe myself,

Very respectfully,

Your friend and servant,

BENJ. F. BUTLER.

www.ingramcontent.com/pod-product-compliance
Lightning Source LLC
LaVergne TN
LVHW011132110826
845150LV00008B/2304
9781418194123